73

Yarmulkes & Fitted Caps
a collection of poetry

ରଃ

by Aaron Levy Samuels

Write Bloody Publishing
America's Independent Press

Austin, TX

WRITEBLOODY.COM

Samuels, Aaron Levy.
1st edition.
ISBN: 978-1938912-38-2

Interior Layout by Lea C. Deschenes
Cover Design & Photography by Lauren Banka
"Man in Tallis" photograph by Mikhail Levit
Author Photo by Jonathan Weiskopf
Proofread by Helen Novielli
Edited by by Laura Yes Yes, Geoff Kagan-Trenchard, Derrick Brown, & Jon Sands

Type set in Bergamo from www.theleagueofmoveabletype.com

Printed in Tennessee, USA

Write Bloody Publishing
Austin, TX
Support Independent Presses
writebloody.com

To contact the author, send an email to writebloody@gmail.com

MADE IN THE USA

For Devin

Yarmulkes & Fitted Caps

Those that don't got it can't show it.
Those that got it can't hide it.
– Zora Neale Hurston

In Jewish history there are no coincidences.
– Elie Wiesel

A lot of people pretty much only listen to the chorus.
– Lenny Kravitz

Yarmulkes & Fitted Caps

WHICH KEEPS ME

Black is the stain on me
that everyone feels
comfortable ignoring.
Jewish is that too.

The water keeps me here;
I am not sure if I want to stay.
When I say rope,
I mean that which coils and unfurls.

When I say Black,
I mean that which is
constant as water.

Water coils and unfurls.

Jewish is that too.
When I say mother, I mean
which keeps me here;
everyone

feels more comfortable ignoring:
Black, the stain, that too.

When I say unfurl, I mean my afro,
Jewfro—it coils
and coils.
When I say keeps me here, I mean

I cut it off, curl by curl. When I say cut
I mean plucked, I mean Jewish;
a stain that everyone feels
comfortable plucking rope by rope.

The water keeps me here.
When I say here,

I mean not here; never was;

a stain
everyone feels more comfortable ignoring,

a rope which coils and unfurls—
remains as constant as water,

which keeps me here,
which brought me here.

Black is that too.
Jewish is that too.
Jewish is Black too.

The stain is the water
is the rope; the curls
are
coils
unfurling
and unfurling

like an afro
like an afro
like an answer
plucked out of the water

Black
by Black.

BORN – *1992*
after Jeanann Verlee

I was born of Edgewood, born of Al-Mall quickie mart
slash hookah bar slash pizza parlor slash ministry, born
of South Providence next door, with their chimi trucks
and speed bumps, called us *edge-hood*, called us *E-dubb*
called us secret handshakes, secret language, from *fachii*,
and *boss-man*, *bogue-rocks*—mom couldn't understand
a damn word—born of Warwick next door, their strip malls
and baseball and long roads, born of Broad Street, Park Ave,
bicycles with pegs to stand on and handle bars to sit—
three to a bike: *no problem*; born between exurb
and ghetto flanks, the water pulling us together
beneath our city, its soft hands, born of Narragansett Bay,
of low tide, of white geese

covered in black oil.

WHAT REALLY HAPPENED ON MT. MORIAH

There was no lamb

struggling in a hidden thicket
horns clawing
the brush;

no angel,

    no gust of wind
    thunder to make the hand

hesitate;

just the blade

just / the throat

    empty.

as the servants watched

their eyes—
a silent covenant

to tell the story

differently.

Why Jewish Kids Ain't White Sometimes

Ayo Aaron, where you from? Where your parents
from? Hola, como estás? Why does your skin tan quicker
than mine? I overheard you saying the N-word so… do
you believe in god? You're not *really* black… you can't
rap? You can rap? Did you learn that from your father?
I thought you would be better at basketball. Wait,
you're not Spanish?
You don't even speak *Spanish*?
or *Hebrew*?
You shouldn't send a picture to your scholarship program.
But is your MOM Jewish? What was the theme
to your Bar Mitzvah?

or Do you *believe* in god?

*My daddy says that all the Jews are gonna go to hell
but I like you so can you come to church with me?*

or *Kike*, don't get offended by the word *kike*.
Nobody uses that word anymore.   *or*

Language is evolving ~~nigger~~ nigga.   *or*

It's ok, there were black kids in my high school;
they told me it was ok.

or

*They don't care about a nigga; them mothafuckers jewed us
out the projects to build an Urban Outfitters.*

or

THAT IS THE BLACKEST JEWISH STAR
I have ever seen.   *or*

Jewbag
Jewtard   Jewey mc duck
                 Jewey mc Jewface
                 Jewfish
                                Jewfucker

or

You're not really Jewish   are you?
You're not really black   right?

Are you *you*?   Are there others?
Are you others
          like you?   Is there anyone else?
Anyone in the world?

Is there any world like you?
Is there any world that likes you?

Broken Ghazal in the Voice
of My Brother Jacob

Irrefutable fact / my brother is black jewish
Kink hair & a wide nose / that's gotta be black, jewish

He said look in the mirror / naked / if it ain't black—jewish
       If we don't do it to ourselves / first / then they do it to us

Said he loves countin' stacks / is that black? / jewish?
Said we loves eating chicken cause we black-jewish!

Said, you gotta keep it real / listen to black music
If you wanna keep your teeth / you ain't allowed to act jewish

And that's jewish / Night of the broken glass jewish
They'll beat your face in with a bat / until its black.

They raped your great-grandma, and that's a fact, jewish
Say a prayer for the secrets your family keeps, Kaddish

See Aaron, you run / but I learned to attack: jewish
       In order to survive, you gotta be black, stupid

Let 'em tattoo my arm, that's how I act jewish
That's how I be black / but that's not what you did

Got yourself a "good job," where nobody's black / jewish
Cut the slang off your tongue / it's too black; jewish

And, you never came home / Aaron / where it's black-jewish
And not coming home / is black
                     jewish

THE BLACK PENIS TALKS SHIT
TO THE REST OF AARON
after Angel Nafis

Got some mayonnaise on your face;
you sun-burned tuna fish, K-Swiss,
Phil-Collins-is-more-gangster-than-you, scrawny
pale broccoli head. Your momma so white

she thought *Strange Fruit* was a smoothie bar, so white
she thought Air Force One was an airplane for
her president, so white, she thought she chose her
president, you cracker barrel.
You Starbucks café.

You sandals and pink shorts Gumby-legs, collar-popped
polo, can-I-offer-you-a-glass-of-white-wine, hockey,
One Tree Hill fucker. And you

want to talk about birthright, as if it's something you
deserved, because of a vagina you were marshmallow
enough to be s'mored through, as if you could take a
Kierkegaard to your genitals and slice away what gutters
you earthworm—you nutless-buttersquash.

Harry-Potter-themed-bar-mitzvah,

sinus medicine, SoBe-Life-Water fucker.
As if you could run away from me
with those white feet, snipe your way to Israel
and forget about me.

I am the 45 in your SPF,
you banker, tourist.
Act like I ain't the triangle in your ocean.
Act like I ain't the pyramids in your deserts.
Act like I ain't built you

with my calloused finger, pointing
always pointing   north.

MIRIAM'S APOLOGY

Not simply because the decree
would have left you a red, wilted rag
in the lap of your mother, your neck

circumcised to the bone—
much more than your survival,
this was for all of us;

your skin just dark enough
to walk unquestioned
along palace walls,

your wrists adorned with gold
instead of leather
or lead.

We thought it was impossible
for someone who looked like us
to sit anywhere near a throne,

someone so easily burned
to drink wine
red as the pyramids at sundown.

A fool's errand really
to believe
all that separated us was a thick wicker weave

& a farm's length of river;
to believe
it was actually that easy

to become a prince.

BORN – SUMMER 1996

In first grade summer camp
the counselors pelican-marched us
to the bamboo & sludge
of the Narragansett Bay,
told us to pick up sea glass.
My mother said
they made a bunch of six-year-olds pick up glass?
We came home with jars full,
softened colored shards,
remnants of broken bottles
left in the salt water.
I kept as much as I could under my bed,
took some out each sundown, ran my fingers
along the edges, tipped my salted tongue
to the top part of the ocean,
pretended to crunch—
take that glass away from your face!
My mother lifted me up by my neck skin,
looked at all of the places I could bleed from,
watched me run barefoot
down the middle of the road
back to an ocean filled with glass.
She called it love, but really
it was a warped and seasoned fear:
that any broken thing would break
again.

JACOB WALKS HOME
FROM THE PROVIDENCE PLACE MALL

If Jacob had been home for dinner,
the brass Jewish star dog tag would have rested
on a full stomach in an Edgewood kitchen,
instead of floating like a buoy

in the dank of his royal blue tall-T.
He marches his Timberlands,
midnight air honking at his legs
through the holes in his older brother's jeans.

Jacob licks at the rolling paper
stuck between his braces,
when the Impala rolls up on him
& shouts in four voices,

> *SOUTHSIDE NIGGA, CRABS DIE!*
> *YOU ALONE HOMIE?*
> *WHERE YOUR CREW AT HOMIE?*
> *WHERE YOU GOING NIGGA?*

But the car drives away
as Jacob ditches the tall-T
in the nearest trash can
& continues his ten mile walk home,

bare-chested,
hands shivering in his pockets—
one holding his cell phone
with ignored calls

from both parents
who he had told earlier that day
that he was cool
that he didn't need a ride home.

PALMALYSIS
definition

noun

1. Condition in which one loses the physical ability to move one's hands; often caused by weakness, fear, confusion, and/or love.

2. Condition in which one loses the desire to move one's hands from their current location, often caused by knowledge that alternate locations are cold, unwelcoming, non-community-oriented, and/or racist.

3. The decision-making process one undertakes when determining whether or not to shake someone's hand—someone witnessed previously using said hand for a disgusting and/or unappealing purpose such as exiting a bathroom without washing, picking a nose or ear, sneezing directly into the palm, striking the face of a stranger, withholding food, withholding water, confiscating necessary belongings, confiscating children, manipulating the stock market, operating a drone combat vehicle, building an internment camp, murder, systemized oppression, genocide, and/or collecting monetary profit from aforementioned acts—forcing one to question the many handshakes one has experienced in one's lifetime, causing a temporary paralysis as one stares at the enveloping digits and wonders what it really means to be clean.

COUSIN DEBORA SHOT HERSELF
in the voice of Jacob

with a gun
in the chest

this morning,

before you woke up.

that's why mom is crying,

she thinks

she could have stopped her,

she thinks

she felt a ghost last night
crawl into her bed

she ignored it

like a cold wind.

our uncle;
he left a loaded gun
under the pillow,

he thinks

he killed her.

Bury Me a Man
for Troy Davis

bury me a man
fix your eyes against my chest
then bury me again

let the public stand
nothing weary rests
bury me a man

appeal to sky, appeal to sand
don't allow the sun to set
then bury me again

a drone, a thousand ants
beneath the rocky sediment
bury me a man

i will come back with cratered hands
unconcerned with innocence
then—i dare you—bury me again

rotted above; will rot as long within
this fertile soil will not forget
they buried me a man
then buried me again.

LETTER FROM OCTAVIA BUTLER
TO RABBI MOSES MAIMONIDES

Dearest Rambam,

You don't know me. But I wanted to tell you, I get it: why you couldn't stop at just one book, because then they call you crazy. But we know better. You have to keep writing until the aliens are angels, until their tentacled skin slides every suction cup right off the binding. Then it's not a story anymore. It's a vampire. Sink your teeth into their eyeballs. Then they will see: it's a nebula, spinning dust all over the library. It's dirty work we do. That's how our skin got so black, do you remember? When you first went back in time?

I took a quill pen and levered it underneath my left foot, pulled it straight out of my nostril. That's how it feels to go back to the mountain where it all started, where you first started etching stories into your tongue. It won't kill you. But that don't make it ok: a whip that is: straight to the lamb's meat of your back. A whole shipment, the tractor beam wasn't big enough for all of those whips, all of those boats and muskets.

We had to walk all the way up the mountain to get them. My feet were covered in blood and babies. But someone had to out-crazy the crazy demon mountain monsters. Someone had to pluck the hairs off of their fingers one by one and draw the stories in the stone. Thank you for the stone.

Thank you for having the audacity to tell the truth! You are a truth teller! You gave me the strength to tell my stories as they actually happened, bleeding every page. We can laugh at them now. Now that they called us geniuses! Who's crazy? Not us. Not when we know how ridiculous it is to be black: so crazy that we must be time-traveling insects. We must be demons and aliens, with green skin and a penchant for symbiosis. We must have stumbled upon two magic stones at the top of a mountain that told us we were the chosen people!

Or else, what other reason could there be? What other way can we justify what happened to us, again, and again? Where could all of those scars possibly have come from?

There is no other explanation.

Yours Forever,
Octavia

Caprice in Elementary

Darlene said you were gay
if you stepped on the purple tiles.
This is true.

I used to jump for this girl, followed her
around the edge of the cafeteria,
never stepping on the purple tiles.

I used to wait for winter to end.

One time an albino boy named Stacy
stepped on purple.
He was a gay boy

gay gay gay gay gay gay gay.
I used to stand still in turtlenecks and watch
but really I used to hide

under orange leaves with my mouth shut
and Stacy used to say *so what if I am!*
And then his nose used to be broken

and leaves used to be stuck
to his body with dried blood & I used
to be skinny and have small hands

and tuck my turtlenecks into dungarees
when the mornings were purple and orange.
The schoolyard was never big enough

so I pulled a skull cap over my black
curls, tied my waist with a braided belt.
I used to be orange tiles in the hallways,

and Stacy used to walk on purple
and be covered in it and I tell this story
and pretend that I used to be Stacy,

used to have iron pipes in my arms,
that I used to walk home every day
with a face covered in brown scabs,

that the New England wind used to remind me
how many entrances there were into my skin,
that I was not a small burrowing creature,

that I was more than a boy who just stood
and watched, more than a pile of leaves
in an Edgewood schoolyard,

that I used to survive the winter.

TEN PLAGUES
after Laura Yes Yes

*And the LORD spake unto Moses, Say unto Aaron, Take thy
rod, and stretch out thine hand upon the waters of Egypt, upon
their streams, upon their rivers, and upon their ponds, and
upon all their pools of water, that they may become blood;
and that there may be blood throughout all the land of Egypt,
both in vessels of wood, and in vessels of stone.*
—Exodus 7:19

Hebrew	דָּם (Dam)
Act of God	Plague of blood
Act of Terror	Cut the water supply

Hebrew	צְפַרְדֵּעַ (Tzfardeiah)
Act of God	Plague of frogs
Act of Terror	Break down the front door

Hebrew	כִּנִּים (Kinim)
Act of God	Plague of lice
Act of Terror	Place black hoods over their faces

Hebrew	עָרוֹב (Arov)
Act of God	Plague of wild animals
Act of Terror	Dare them to try and sleep

Hebrew	דֶּבֶר (Dever)
Act of God	Plague of pestilence
Act of Terror	Burn their prayer books

Hebrew	שְׁחִין (Shkhin)
Act of God	Plague of boils
Act of Terror	Piss on the bandages

Hebrew	בָּרָד (Barad)
Act of God	Plague of hail
Act of Terror	Launch a metal flock into the sky

Hebrew	אַרְבֶּה (Arbeh)
Act of God	Plague of locusts
Act of Terror	Make them fear the quiet buzz

Hebrew	חוֹשֶׁךְ (Choshech)
Act of God	Plague of darkness
Act of Terror	Strike quickly

Hebrew	מַכַּת בְּכוֹרוֹת (Makat B'Chorot)
Act of God	Death of the firstborn
Act of Terror	Do whatever it takes to be free

Free to Choose

In eighth grade the mayor visited our school
to lecture us about the "choice" program.

All students in Cranston were free to choose
their high school—Cranston West or Cranston East—

regardless of our district. The school system
drove buses with us Eastside boys across the city,

away from Elmwood Ave. and Broad Street.
We watched out of windows as the "ethnic food"

changed from Cambodian to Italian—
talking shit the whole time, free-styling, Damien:

My name is Dommy D, all the girls be feeling me
I punch you in the face, you be saying OOO EEE

Said *my older brother goes to East,*
my mom went to East, Fuck the West.

Fuck their Nissan Muranos
and their fancy soccer cleats.

We don't need that shit;
we had our own concrete.

We didn't want their groomed grass,
their "vocational school"

And the mayor knew.
Nobody was bused here from the West Side.

If they wanted to come across the city
to buy a Black & Mild, or fuck an East Side girl

they would gel their hair to the left side,
grab a cashmere pullover from the closet

hop in the car dad bought them
for their sixteenth birthday—

smelling of peppermint
and Axe body spray—

bring the engine to a slow quiet growl
and drive.

JACOB TAUGHT ME

the way a *wu-banger* is created:
rolling a blunt & sprinkling cocaine
front to back across the leaves.   he taught me
this. taught me snorting would leave your septum
freckled with white scratches, like Old Dirty,
like a brown duck sinking into the bay,
but smoking—different, only scratch inside.
you can be black as night, no one would know.
taught me the whiteness inside feels like all
the light switches in my mind were turned up.
our vibrating skull makes the high different
every time; that's why this whiteness is so
addictive;   because we need to know
what the shadows look like with the lights on.

THE JEWISH PENIS TALKS SHIT
TO THE REST OF AARON
for Kevin Coval

I took your money, ate it
like it was made of golden chocolate—it was;
soaked it in batter and potatoes.

I nibbled on it by candlelight.
You're a bad prayer,
a mourners' kaddish without a minyan.

You're a curly haired schmuck at the JCC
after-school program.
Jealous choir boy, doughy

stuffed into your button down;
your pants are way too tight.
That's why you have no friends.

You're the forty-fifth candle
in the Chanukah box,
the weak foot that can't break the wedding glass.

You can read Hebrew
but you don't know what the damn words mean.
You're a sukkah in a rainstorm.

I came to your Saturday morning service,
threw candy at you on the bima,
watched your eye pop out of its socket,

roll down the open Torah, watched
the cantor try to catch it in his tallis.
I tweeted about it, right away.

I put superglue in your yarmulke,
raised your rent,
turned your heat on in the summer

put your tefillin in my lunch box,
got mayonnaise all over
the straps.

I went to Israel for free,
unzipped at the Western Wall;
I left a wet message on the Kotel.

I tied your shoelaces together;
everyone watched
as you nosedived into the wall.

Some thought you stumbled
at the sight
of so much wailing.

Others thought
you were overcome
with prayer.

But as your knees hit the stone floor
and your head plummeted
into your thighs,

I knew
you were bowing
to me.

Mom Explains the Events that Took Place after Her Father Died

baby, there is no god but they'll kill you for him.
—Daphne Gottlieb

After your grandfather died we sat shiva.
Your aunt
held her own shiva at the same time.
No one came to mine.

Left me with the body, though,
rotting and filled with smoke.
So I did what any good daughter would do:
buried it.
Found a small plot of land and a casket I could afford
and lowered him into the earth.

It wasn't over though.
They came back
with shovels in hand.
Said they bought a family plot
in the rich Jewish cemetery
with the bodies mapped out in a family tree.
Said they needed him to fill his place.

Told the groundskeeper they would have him
out in no time—
not on my watch.
I stood on top of that grave for weeks
with my own weapons.
Had to hire my own Jewish lawyer to fight with theirs.

We had to file a restraining order for a dead man!
Ain't that
some shit.

Like a good daughter, I put his body in the ground.
And like a good daughter
I made sure it never came out.

TOTEM: MALCOLM X DOG TAG

When I was fourteen I got a dog tag chain
with Malcolm X at the end of it—a totem
to remind the world how black

I was. Malcolm X was the blackest person
I knew, except maybe Denzel Washington
but then again, well, you know.

I figured that as long as I wore this chain
nobody could steal my blackness from me.
Before Malcolm, people used to just help themselves.

Used to reach into my thighs, the blackest body part
I owned and grab a fistful; watch it pour like ash
into the atmosphere—a cloud of high top sneakers,

and claps on 2 & 4. When it was gone,
they would act like it didn't just happen
like there wasn't ash underneath their white nails,

tried to play it off, in their full body velour jumpsuits
tucked into Timbs. They'd be like:
you're not even all the way black

like that wasn't the same as reaching into the meat
of my other thigh. But with Malcolm around my neck
they couldn't touch me. I tested it out:

put my chain on over my cornrows & watched
the fist slowly un-punch my nose,
a thick maroon stream creeping into my left nostril.

The books flung themselves into my backpack,
which was ripped right onto my shoulders
when I ran towards the group of boys

waiting for me after school.
After they un-jumped me,
we all gave each other daps

the way black boys do—
one hand extended to meet the quivering embrace,
the other clutching the black Malcolm

on my chest, just so the world knew
I wasn't dreaming.

Rules

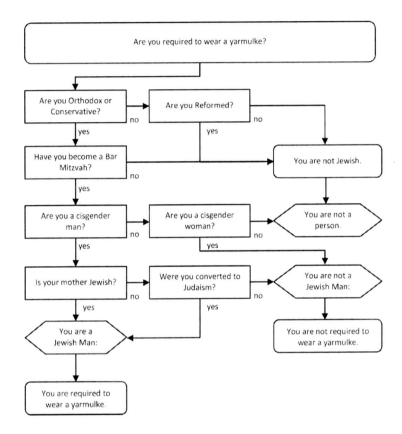

Are you required to wear a yarmulke?

Are you Orthodox or Conservative? — no → Are you Reformed? — no → You are not Jewish.

Are you Orthodox or Conservative? — yes → Have you become a Bar Mitzvah?

Are you Reformed? — yes

Have you become a Bar Mitzvah? — no → You are not Jewish.

Have you become a Bar Mitzvah? — yes → Are you a cisgender man?

Are you a cisgender man? — no → Are you a cisgender woman?

Are you a cisgender woman? — no → You are not a person.

Are you a cisgender man? — yes → Is your mother Jewish?

Are you a cisgender woman? — yes → Were you converted to Judaism?

Is your mother Jewish? — no → Were you converted to Judaism?

Were you converted to Judaism? — no → You are not a Jewish Man:

You are not a Jewish Man: → You are not required to wear a yarmulke.

Is your mother Jewish? — yes → You are a Jewish Man:

Were you converted to Judaism? — yes → You are a Jewish Man:

You are a Jewish Man: → You are required to wear a yarmulke.

ASSIMILATION

My mother has no idea

where I went during temple.
There was a secret door behind the small chapel;
it led to Blockbuster—

I ate Sour Patch Watermelons during all eighteen
of my classmates' Bar Mitzvahs.
Nobody could find me.

I had armpits that grew payos before my face could.
I pulled them out; Scotch-taped them to my cheeks,
never showed anyone the pictures.

I wore it on my chest:
a star tucked into an undershirt
in a middle school locker room.

I kicked my way through the hallways,
saved allowance for an entire year
to buy my first pair: Air Force One mid-tops.

I walked through the holy sanctuary
like a duck;
my shoelaces were anchors.

I had friends who knew who I was
Jewish, just
wanted to know I was black first.

I tucked my yarmulke into my suit pocket
every Saturday
before my friends gave me daps

on my walk home.

INTEGRATION

My grandfather treated his Jamaica
like an accent
he taught my father to not use,

tucked his shirt in each morning—
his corporate uniform a pristine onyx,
not a wrinkle until he was back in his own bedroom.

My grandfather came to this country
a pumice stone, slapped the island
off of my father's tongue.

He polished my father until the neighborhood
could see its reflection in his black shining skin;
smoothed every aperture, filled each pore.

My grandfather never went back over the water.

PROMISES

*Insanity is doing the same thing over and over
again and expecting different results.*
–Albert Einstein

I looked up to smart people, like my cousin Debora.
She promised she would never do anything to hurt me.
I asked her, why? She said it would be insane

to love me any other way. She killed herself
when she was 14. So I found other people to look up to,
like my parents—they always kept their promises—

made me and my little brother Jacob keep our promises too.
He was three years younger than me. He picked his nose
and loved to eat jawbreakers.

And I was smart, and cared about people. I kept my promises.
And Debora told me that according to Einstein,
an electron could exist and not exist at the same time.

That was crazy. But Debora kept doing the same things
over and over and that didn't help her parents
fall back in love, or keep their promises,

or be more like my parents, who told Jacob and me
that Debora shot herself with her father's gun,
and that she did it on purpose.

Then I promised I would never do that; Jacob promised too.
And I promised to stay in school; Jacob promised too.
And I promised to always keep my promises.

Jacob promised too.
We kept our promises
in this family.

Jacob dropped out of school in sixth grade.
I didn't look up to him.
Then he almost dropped out of a window.

I didn't look up to that either. But I had to promise
to forgive him, because families promise to forgive
each other. But that didn't make any sense

because then he would do the same thing over and over
and he dropped out of school in seventh grade, and dropped
into a doctor's office, who said,

> *Bipolar is a brain disorder that causes*
> *unusual shifts in mood, energy,*
> *and the ability to keep promises.*

According to Einstein, I am crazy, and Jacob
is the opposite of crazy because he did the same thing
every day and got different results—crazy,

people trying to keep their promises,
waking up each morning searching, always searching
for electrons, disappearing in our microscopes.

Jacob, there was a time I promised I'd never end up like you;
doing the same thing over and over
and never knowing the results;

and there was a time I promised I'd never end up like you;
doing the same thing over and over
and never knowing the results;

and there was a time I promised I'd never end up like you
and we keep our promises
in this family.

Translating Jacob

I watched him cut open a rock with his teeth.
There were twenty emerald mountaintops trapped inside,
scratching at the walls with their knuckles, which means

there is always a chance for escape.
The escape means I don't feel at home anywhere;
our bedrooms had windows too high to land from.

The holes in his wall mean he is strong: a tree trunk
crawling towards the edge of the sidewalk.
The white walls mean he is not strong

enough, that even a rock can become its own prisoner.
His eyes mean that there will always be colors
I cannot see. *Jacob* means I will never be alone,

his face means my face
will always have a companion,
his cornrows mean I had cornrows two years prior,

means he had to wait
until he wasn't copying me. *His clothing*
means my clothing, heavy, baggy, fits neither of us—

perfect. *He* means *I*. *Jacob* will always mean I
can never leave. *Again*—means I already left
years ago,

Jacob, his body in a locked room; it doubled in size
in four weeks, his body that is. *Delayed metabolism*
means he swallowed twenty little mountaintops

each day; they bring them in a small plastic rock
with water. *Visit* means I might not come back,
means my brother might not come back. *I'm sorry*

means I will come back at least one more time;
our skin is connected: a stretched wire
rope between our eyes—

glistening geodes, hair quartz and calcite.
Jacob means if you abandon something long enough,
it may harden into something beautiful,

a polished stone.

Born – Broad Street, Winter 2001

I was not born   in   Edgewood   no one is born
in Edgewood   but we move and settle
until the water and salt harden us   scabbed fist in my pocket
bag of peas in my freezer   born of Edgewood   where
the hardest out was the boy who could take the most punches
still smile sea salt the next day   born of America   Online CDs
in bulk   stolen from Wal-Mart   and garage doors
to tape them to   bb guns to shoot them with

born of pornography   Kevin's divorced father left it in the
VCR   we made fun of the first one to get a boner   and the
last   it was unanimously agreed that it was cool   because
everyone had their own blanket   it was definitely not gay

born of the poker game on Friday night in the basement of
Kevin's house   Kevin had bought a bike from a boy
named Jimmy behind Luchetti's restaurant while I
kept lookout   when the poker game gossip told us Jimmy had
sold us a stolen bike   we pelican-marched to the other side of
town   took the money back   Edgewood style,
we kept the bike, smoked *bogue-rocks* in our triumph
boss-man

I won poker that winter night   called *fachii*   walked home
with a pocket full of seventy five dollars   my dick folded up behind
      my belt loop   ears tucked into a fitted cap
a silver Star of David salting my neck   shining in the midnight
like stained glass

SHABBAT SHALOM:
THE COOLEST JEWISH KID EVER

He wore a lot of baby blue. Tar Heels jersey.
North Carolina headband:
cloud white & light blue detail.

Kicks glide, toe slides, heel up kick,
weight shift, moon walk backwards. Pivot.
Joseph always had a basketball with him.

My best friend: quick steps. We'd joke
his hair was nappy-er than mine—it was.
Both Jewish, me Black, also.

Joseph brushed his hair before basketball games,
JCC league, *Tom Brady gels his hair
before Patriots' games.* So he did too

before ping pong games, before U.S.Y. dances
never missed a step. Fake Air Force Ones—
nobody noticed—as he'd cross up

every middle school gangster on the court.
His signature move: fake left, behind the back, jump,
under the leg   dunk (maybe)

Shabbat Shalom Mothafucka!

Watch the shoulders, pop lock, confident. Joseph
had mad game, always had a girlfriend.
A bagel in one hand,

never cream cheese in his braces.

FIRE/(FLY):
THE COOLEST BLACK KID EVER

Damien only got my name right one time—
when the sky was dark blue, sun flickering

in the evening above Carberry Field—
at this precise time, when Damien would shed

his grey du-rag and white tall-T to the sideline,
when fireflies began to come out of the grass

when superstars became high schoolers
again, and bullies became momma's boys—

that is when Damien and his team
finally needed an extra man.

His hands buzzing through the evening wind
he would call for the rock

and laser beam it at my lack of a chest:
Aaron, you in nigga?

★

When I come home from college four years later
I see Damien at Carberry, dribbling on the concrete.

Hair no longer braided,
surrounding his face like an exoskeleton,

sneakers peeling from the bottoms of his feet,
the court filled mostly with stragglers

and Damien flying around everyone
like blades of grass.

His eyes meet mine across the Carberry twilight
and I knew he could see, clear as the sweat on my nose,

that there was a time I would have traded
every book I owned to have wings like his,

as the fireflies danced around the grass blades
and the momma's boys walked their tired asses home.

Special Delivery:
the Blackest Jewish Kid Ever
after Jon Sands

It is the last 5 minutes of Hebrew School dance class.
Your teacher shuts off the 1937 version
of *Ushavtem Mayim B'sason*,

gives the nod of approval to Benjamin Zipperstein.
He turns up the best possible dance track:
Special Delivery off Bad Boy's *We Invented the Remix*

& you are no longer the sticky-haired nerd boy
trapped in Hebrew School in Edgewood.
You are the half Black half Jewish love child

of Usher and Michael Jackson.
That's what your middle school friends told you.
That's where you learned the secret formula

to anything and everything cool: melanin—
the most badass chemical on the planet!
That's where you learned:

when an octopus is being attacked by a predator
it launches a cloud of liquid melanin into the ocean
as it escapes. True story!

& you know the truth of this story just as you know the black
liquid running currents through your shaking body
the moment you are commanded to dance.

This is when you show all your Jewish friends
that your blackness is a bag of Orville Redenbacher's
and the dance floor is the microwave!

Last time your corduroys split right down the middle.
But this time you are ready. You got your 100% Polyester grey
and white Adidas swishies,

got your P. Diddy battle track,
got your yarmulke AND your fitted cap.
Both match your sneakers.

& you are an octopus.   Music pulls your body
in eight directions & your friends want you to dance so bad,
they don't realize they have become sharks,

their white teeth clapping to the beat
& you dig from inside your gut and launch
a smoke cloud of blackness into the synagogue

& suddenly everything you do
is the blackest dance move possible.

    The sideways karate chop *black*.
    The life size soup bowl *black*.

    They ask you if you can Crip walk, you say *yes*.
    They ask you if you can Harlem shake, you say *yes*.

    They ask you if you can do a windmill,
    then pivot quickly to a head spin pop! You say *YES*.

Because you are that black!
While everyone else burns, you just get blacker.
Black is the new Jewish & Jewish is the new Black

& you are the Blackest Jewish Kid in Edgewood.

Kahlil Gibran Helps Aaron Reconcile the Black Penis and the Jewish Penis
with apologies to Kahlil Gibran

Your Black Penis is your Jewish Penis unmasked.
And the selfsame well from which your laughter rises

was oftentimes filled with your tears.
And how else can it be?

The deeper that Jewish Penis carves into your being,
the more Black Penis you can contain.

Is not the cup that holds your wine
the very cup that was burned in the potter's oven?

And is not the lute that soothes your spirit,
the very wood that was hollowed with knives?

When you are a Black Penis, look deep into your heart
and you shall find

it is only that which has given you your Jewish Penis
that is giving you your Black Penis.

When you are a Jewish Penis
look again in your heart,

and you shall see that in truth you are weeping
for that which has been your delight.

Some of you say, "The Black Penis is greater
than the Jewish Penis,"

and others say, "Nay, The Jewish Penis is the greater."
But I say unto you, they are inseparable.

Together they come, and when one sits
alone with you at your board,

remember that the other is asleep
upon your bed.

Verily, you are suspended like scales
between your Jewish Penis and your Black Penis.

Only when you are empty
are you at a standstill and balanced.

When the treasure-keeper lifts you
to weigh his gold and his silver,

your body, alas,
more than a glimmering spectacle,

behold as your Black Penis
and your Jewish Penis

rise
and fall.

PETER IS DEAD AND I AM A MOTORCYCLE

A motorcycle is on my sweater. I am thirteen.
My sweater has yellow sleeves the color of real fire
& Peter's face is a headlight projecting on the screen.

People walk up to a microphone, one by one, to remember.

I think that I must be a motorcycle.
The lights are off. My eyes are spinning rubber
& I keep balance by moving as fast as I can.

The only visible things in the auditorium,
besides Peter's face, are my sleeves, glowing
like an accident, an ember that I wish I could destroy.

But you can't kill fire.
You have no control over what gets to die.
I just have to take things as they come:

> I play the sports my father played,
> I do my homework,
> I try to fit in,

& I knew I was a Kawasaki,
yellow and cutting through wind
like Peter's hair.

He was seventeen, the most beautiful motorcycle on the road,
the type that would make out with the lead girl
behind the stage during intermission, then explain

to all the curious twelve-year-olds what love is.
He taught himself guitar, then made a rock band
from every garage in the neighborhood, invited you

to his party, where he played guitar,
convinced your parents that you were safe there.
He had no idea

that the nightclub would catch fire the night of his first show,
the roof would collapse while he was on stage,
that his face would become an auditorium

of rusty cars and skateboards and people
who did not want to see real fire, yellow and burning
like a final performance,

like a thirteen-year-old
who didn't know what a mentor was
until I looked at the fire on my own sleeves, realized

that I was raining on them, and stopped.
Because I was in a black room
but I was the roaring engine of a motorcycle,

alive and spinning
yellow as the flames
in Peter's eyes.

Kevin Convinced Me to Drink

the bottle, a brown eyeball daring me to blink.
I was fourteen and unsure how I felt about white people
but I knew I didn't like beer.

Kevin was white, and liked beer. He said
it's what men do. *They drink beer and watch sports
and get into fights or else they are a pussy.*

I remember thinking this must be racist in a way
against women. I had never seen a pussy before
or any type of vagina, but I knew what a pussy was

from the movies we all watched at Kevin's house.
In seventh grade, Brandon took off everything
except his sneakers, chased us around the house,

a beer in one hand, his pinkish-white genitals
in the other. We ran around screaming and laughing
while he called us gay and threatened to cream on us.

I giggled and said that must be racist
against gay people and probably women.
And we ate hot pockets.

Kevin grabbed a couple *brewskies* from his dad's stash,
said *you don't seem that black to me,*
and punched me in the chest.

THE WORST PARTS OF LOVE
after Jeanann Verlee

It's been a year since we dated and she still loves me
and she trusts my smile and I just woke up from a long
nap and my sweatpants are a storefront window and my
erection is pressing its face against the glass and "come
over to watch a movie" means "come over to have sex"
(everybody knows this) and the shades are closed and
the theater is a twin sized dorm room bed and the laptop
is a heated blanket across our thighs and she says
she "only wants to be friends" and I know she means it
and I am not sure if I ever loved her and I tell her
that I miss kissing her and she tells me to stop and
her sweatpants are a storefront window and she shakes
her head and she does not smile and I do not move
and she presses her lips against my face and I do not move
and my face is my chest and my chest is in between
my thighs and her naked body is a red heated blanket
and the movie is over and I ask her if it was good
and she says yes and does not look at me and I feel
like I have stolen something and I blame her and I curse
her silence under my breath as she walks across
my bedroom and I blame her for ruining everything and
I blame her for not wanting me but still taking my fingers,
for placing them inside her and I am the villain
with deep eyes and a hunger and the power to turn
lights off and the power to stare at a window until
the glass shatters, until she walks across it, the power
to blame her for this too; for looking at this monster
that I keep locked in my room and loving him still,
every tooth, wearing my smile like a storefront, slipping
onto my body like a pair of sweatpants.

PULLING

A place underneath my skin contains
my first touches. I forgot most. I lost
your eyelash, and I would have kept pulling
them from you—each penny a tear duct.
There are women who make you feel guilty,
dad said, and then there are men. But you,
me: two cygnets wrapped in patchwork. Gentle
memories are first to go. I was standing
on my hands; I desired a few long years
inside your laughter, which is your cheekbone
touch. I hope I can return to that place;
in darkness I imagine your eyelash
waiting. It is. I am sure—this is all
I know of love at the edge of winter.

WHEN MOSES STAYED
for Moses's black wife

My people wither, Zipporah.
Their fair skin crackles in the Egyptian heat,
sweat curling by their ears.

How can I return to a slave people

who eat crackers and play with snakes?
How can I return to such ugly
when I know this now—

the black
faults on your brow line, the desert

scavengers your skin has tamed?

The Multiracial Asian German Woman

who is destructively attractive, tells me
because my mother is Jewish, I don't really count
as Black. In her country, Germany—

not Taiwan, where her mother is from—
everyone just treats her as German.
People aren't "mixed."

A bead of cabernet escapes her mouth.

She says
there is not much diversity in Germany

with no wind—
a well-rehearsed answer:

> *Yes I am sorry.*
> *No, my family did not have any involvement.*
> *Everyone in the whole country*
> *feels really bad about what happened.*

She swills, sips a thick red glass, smiles,
& says words like *Dachau* and *iPhone*.

My face is a Molotov cocktail.
Each freckle: a concentration camp
joke. Each curve: a shipping route.

Her mouth is a train car. My grandmother's face
poking through its enamel bars.
Maroon liquid rises to the cabin roof.

I WATCHED

Kevin, my white best friend,
call someone a nigger.

He said

> *Slavery was a long time ago.*
> *Get over it.*

That night
he helped me with my science homework.
I told him I loved him.

I did.

WHY MOSES LEFT
for Moses's black wife

I watched a sheep die today.
Its pupils shrank and it collapsed
right into a thicket.

There it was, a still creature
covered in wool and sweat—
a staff-rod away from the watering hole.

The flies started to eat its belly

       so I burned it.

TASHLIKH

*Ceremony: On Rosh ha-Shana, Jews go to a river and
symbolically cast their sins, sometimes represented by
bread crumbs, into the water*
—Jewish Literacy by Rabbi Joseph Telushkin

The bread was porous and full of bay water, buoy-like and sacred.
The dock was semi-solid, a plasma anchored to an unclear source.
We were Jewish wanderers, repaying our debt of manna to the
swimming birds, to the water which cleans everything.

The Jacob inside the Jacob who was to breathe naked amongst the
lily-roots, held squid magic, braided carelessly through his cornrows,
dangling across his shoulders like drifting silhouettes on the
mountains between Sinai and Masada. The dock was full of Jewish
families, with bread in our hands and rams' horns quivering on our
lips—a god signal for the water birds, and the other birds, and the
Jews who had acquired too many bread crumbs over the last year.

In our old language there was less difference between bread, and sin,
and god, but I don't know our old language. Grandma threw it in
the water with her bread crumbs.

So I took the hollowed ram's horn and blew an apology into the
water, rippling all of the vowels hidden beneath the trembles in my
words. My people have named the horn a Shofar, and have been
blowing it so long that we argue over the reason why.

Jacob held my Shofar and his, tried to squeeze them into the front
pockets of his broken autumn jacket. We had hollowed the Shofars
ourselves when we were children, soaked in soap water until the
bone slid out from inside the horn, sanded by hand for hours, carved
a mouth-sized hole with a band saw, only removed them from
safekeeping once a year to blow on this sacred day.

Jacob leaned over the beckoning water throwing his sins away one
crumb at a time. I told him that he was too close to the water and
that the Shofars would fall. He ignored me. And he will be my
stubborn younger brother forever. And I knew that I would always

be disappointed in him. And more and more bread crumbs appeared in my pockets each second the horns lay there.

We all heard the plop and bubble of something not bread-like plummeting into the mud water, my pocket now overflowing with bread crumbs, yeasting in brown tufts, crawling from my fingernails and gathering around my fists, our Shofars—the only connection to our mountains—gurgling in the sin water with the birds who had given up flight.

But when I looked at the dock again, his fins and scales had already taken form as if the eternal light inside of Jacob's underwear had blown and rippled away the fabric connecting him to this world. And inside this Jacob, a smaller Jacob, unflinchingly dove naked off of the dock, and disappeared beneath the brown toxic water cloud.

The next chapter none of us expected—

Jacob's braids, black and woven strong like tentacles, a genesis emerging from the bay swamp. His teenage body, as if covered in scales, as if immune to the clouded toxic liquid, climbing triumphantly onto the dock, a ram's horn in each hand and bread crumbs falling to his feet.

I imagined him a fourteen year old boy with cornrows. I imagined him skinny and fragile and guilty, and willing to jump into any sludge puddle to avoid his brother's disappointment.

But we all saw a squid titan, a Moses of sorts, presenting the ram's horn to his people like commandments, standing in a puddle of bread crumbs, happy to have something to blow about.

BORN – EDGEWOOD, WEDNESDAY AFTERNOON, MARCH 2004

The last time I left Kevin's house,
he spray painted the word Jew
on his basement wall,

then announced to the room
he had fucked my ex-girlfriend
as he threw a paint can at my nose,

dared me to do something.

After he said mercy and I pulled
my thumbs from his neck,
he punched the back of my head,

grabbed the metal chain
around my throat; forced my face
into his wooden stairs.

When I clawed out of Kevin's house
dirty and covered in blood;
the sun swept into my eyes

as I saw Edgewood
for the first time.

COVERED IN GRASS

Pauper's field: an unmarked plot of land
where slaves and peasants were buried free of charge

I wear a t-shirt that says an African Proverb
however far a river flows it never forgets its source

I am connected like many Black Americans
I cannot trace my roots far the farthest I can follow
my Black side my living roots
is Brooklyn New York

in Ancient Egypt burial rites determine status
Slaves were not in the afterlife
afforded this luxury left in unmarked graves
they are smooth now covered with grass
as if swept away in the Nile River

I wear a Jewish star my people are
around my neck slaves in Egypt
I am connected like many Jews
to my Jewish side can only trace roots
to Russia to genocide
via New York in New York

it is rumored hundreds of pauper's fields
slave bones beneath the surface
smooth now covered with grass
my past has been swept into
the Hudson river

my mom's grandfather my dad's great grandmother
he is from Russia migrated to Brooklyn
watched his family her family chattel
raped by soldiers again and again
as he hid under the bed I do not know where
I do not know if their parents were buried

there is something intentional
about the not knowing a lack of headstones
in my family tree an absence of memories
my race my religion
makes me need to wear a Jewish star
a t-shirt evidence
of what came before me my family
came to New York with no ties
with chains around their necks
no history my family
but the stars Jewish
around their necks Black
a home does not have headstones
swept into rivers covered in grass
a memory a burden
who died for me to breathe
tongues cut out from Brooklyn
thrown off slave ships from Egypt

the history of my people a pauper's field
I am the headstone
Plantations smooth now
Pyramids covered in grass
I am ghetto I am ghetto
I am Nile I am Hudson

these rivers flow into me
they are my source I cannot forget

WHILE WAITING FOR THE MESSIAH

I chat with the other people waiting—

Jews: with lawn chairs and lemonade,
waiting so long they seem not to care.

Black folk: going to work, perhaps.
Most know that he came already,
didn't pick them up.
They'll wait for the next one.

While I wait, I chat with my dead grandma.

She says *the messiah might not be a man,*
so I should be careful who I fall in love with.

She laughs.

Some of us are pretty sure
the messiah is coming back
and some of us are pretty sure Elvis is too.

Aaron you don't really believe in God do you?
Look around, look at all the silly people
waiting.

But Grandma, I say,
how can so many people be wrong?

How is it possible for this many people
to be wrong?

MY GRANDMA

My Grandma kick the shit out of your grandma.
My Grandma thorough. My Grandma laser-vision.
What's a laser? My Grandma not sure
but she got 'em. Got a Sega Genesis too,
don't need it, but good to have around
when you got grandkids.

My Grandma got grandkids,
got regular kids too.
They're grown up kids, but she still got 'em,
keeps 'em close, like her New York Times.
If anything My Grandma got news:
new news, mostly old news
which I think ain't news no more,
but Grandma says *news is history*.

My Grandma got history,
keeps it in a filing system—
some for every day of the week, with water, and bread.
My Grandma ain't always had water and bread
but fuck it, My Grandma got 'em now,
got a teacher's pension
and a paintbrush. My Grandma paint any world she want.
My Grandma don't make a mess,
just spreads out her history to catch the colors that fall.

My Grandma got colors,
got ugly ones from Grandpa.
My Grandma got the bad end of some bad days from Grandpa.
My Grandma kick the shit out of Grandpa.
Fuck Grandpa, My Grandma kick the shit out of any ugly,
see right through it, and that's love too: a laser.

My Grandma got love too
not for this world though, but
my Grandma live in any world she want.

Fuck any world, my Grandma live in every world!
And I'm her son sometimes and her husband sometimes,
and her grandson sometimes, and it's complicated,
'cause I just came over to play Sega.

My Grandma got Sega.

> *I know Grandma, you told me.*
> *Yea Grandma, you told me.*
> *I got the New York Times right here Grandma.*
> *No Grandma you haven't read this one yet.*

My Grandma ain't read this one yet—
too many memories,
not much room for more.
That's ok.
My Grandma got a lot of good ones,

gave me some too.
Took both legs off her hips one day,
handed them to me,
said I'd get more use from them,
I will.

My Grandma took her eyes out,
drained them in the kitchen &
pulled a thin dripping canvas
from the sink.

She said *don't be afraid Aaron, this is your family,*
and when you got family, who needs money, or God?

My Grandma got money,
and God—
don't believe in either.
My Grandma going to heaven
anyways.

How to Tell Your Story

Your grandma dies
a wrinkled ivory canvas
in a tarnished wooden box.

Your suicidal cousin—
her chest was bleeding years before
she put a bullet inside it.

Your childhood mentor—
only fitting that he die with both hands on a guitar
as the room disappeared into smoke.

Jews don't believe in heaven,
technically,
but one commentary speaks of two mountains
at opposite ends of the afterlife,
each with an angel standing at the peak.

When you die, they sling your soul
back and forth for the rest of time:
a fading line of smoke
in the night sky.

One day your brother will jump from a third story window
and the ground will open like a grandmother's arms,
paint his body red and brown,

& send him on his way.

GLOSSARY OF TERMS

GLOSSARY OF TERMS

Bar Mitzvah: Jewish coming of age ceremony, traditionally for men at age thirteen

bima (or bimah): the stage in a Jewish temple

bogue-rocks: cigarettes (Edgewood vernacular)

boss-man: the highest available trump card; exclamatory statement of victory (Edgewood vernacular)

cantor: Jewish song leader

claps on 2 & 4: refers to the beat count that is clapped or snapped to by people with natural rhythm

crabs: derogatory word for a member of the Crip gang

Dachau: one of the first concentration camps to open in Germany

Edgewood (slang: E-dubb): Rhode Island neighborhood in eastern Cranston bordering Providence to the north, Warwick to the southwest, and the Narragansett Bay to the east.

fachii: perversion of the Italian word for face, *faccia*; exclamatory statement of victory (Edgewood vernacular)

fitted cap: non-adjustable baseball-style hat often associated with the style of young African American men

JCC: Jewish Community Center

kaddish: central Jewish prayer praising God's name; the mourners' kaddish is said as part of Jewish mourning rituals

Kotel (or ha-Kothel): the Jewish designation of the Western Wall or Wailing Wall which is a remnant of the ancient wall that once surrounded the historical Jewish Temple in Jerusalem

Masada: mountain in Israel housing a fortress that was the site of the Jewish mass suicide during the siege of the Roman Empire during the Jewish-Roman Wars (66-136 CE)

minyan: quorum of ten Jewish adults required for religious obligations that require communal prayer

Mt. Moriah: mountain in the book of Genesis that served as the location for the sacrifice of Isaac

Night of the Broken Glass (or Kristallnacht): name of a series of coordinated attacks against Jews throughout Germany and Austria on the night of November 9, 1938

pauper's field: an unmarked plot of land where slaves and peasants were buried free of charge

payos (or payot): hairstyle composed of curly side-locks often worn by Orthodox and Hasidic Jews

schmuck: pejorative Yiddish word meaning penis; used to describe a detestable person

Shabbat Shalom: common Jewish Sabbath greeting; Hebrew for Peace on the Sabbath

shiva: the week-long mourning period in Judaism following the loss of an immediate relative

shofar: Jewish horn, traditionally from a ram, used for religious purposes on Rosh Hashanah and Yom Kippur

Special Delivery: song by rapper G. Dep on Bad Boy Records largely attributed to the popularization of the Harlem Shake dance

sukkah: temporary hut that Jews sleep and celebrate in during the holiday of Sukkot

tallis: Jewish prayer shawl

Tashlikh: ceremony during Rosh Hashanah when Jews cast bread into the river to repent for their sins

tefillin: set of small leather boxes containing sacred Jewish scrolls that Jews wear during weekday morning prayers

Timbs: abbreviation for Timberland boots

Torah: the Jewish Bible including the five books of Moses

Ushavtem Mayim B'sason: classic Israeli folk dance commemorating the discovery of water in the desert

U.S.Y. (United Synagogue Youth): a United States Jewish Youth group

wu-banger: a blunt rolled with marijuana laced with cocaine, popularized by the Wu-Tang Clan

yarmulke: skullcap worn by Jewish males especially during prayer

Zipporah (or Tzipora): the name of Moses's black wife

APPENDIX

APPENDIX

Author's Statement:

This appendix was inspired by Geoff Kagan-Trenchard's *Murder Stay Murder* and Nick Flynn's *The Ticking is the Bomb*.

The poems in this book come as a byproduct of growing up in the Black and Jewish communities that nurtured my growth as an individual, and the literary communities that pushed my development as a writer. I hope that these poems will be used to facilitate more conversations about identity in classrooms, workshops, and discussion groups. In this appendix I have included detailed references for each of my poems as well as suggested writing prompts and conversation topics that can accompany this work. The writing workshops can be used in conjunction with the identity discussions or each can be used independently. Some conversations that result from these prompts may be extremely difficult and involve topics that not all facilitators are prepared to handle. For questions about specific poems or about how to use this work as part of a larger writing curriculum or workshop series, feel free to contact me at AaronSamuelsPoetry.com.

Best,
Aaron

Notes for using the appendix:

Many poems in my book are influenced by the fantastic work of other artists. Under References I have listed poems that directly influenced my work, as well as poems and other sources that work well when using this work for writing workshops and discussions.

The writing prompts included are meant to be a springboard. When teaching, please feel free to expand or change prompts as you see fit for your curriculum.

For identity discussions, please keep a wide definition in mind of what constitutes an identity category; avoid binaries and be open to identity categories you may not expect. Some identity categories include, but are not limited to: gender, sex, race, ethnicity, sexual orientation, religion/faith, social class, age, ability, body type, nationality, citizenship, indigenous affiliation, and education level/type.

*Facilitators should keep in mind that each of these poems has the potential to act as a trigger. For the poems with a stronger risk, I did not include an identity discussion prompt. I would recommend not using these poems for identity conversations unless you are specifically running a curriculum around death, trauma, loss, emotional disorders and are a trained professional in dealing with these issues. If you would still like to run a discussion around one of these poems, please contact me at **AaronSamuelsPoetry.com**.*

Poems listed in alphabetical order.

Assimilation

<u>Writing Workshop</u>: When did you feel like you had to hide one identity in order to protect the integrity of another identity? What did that feel like? What steps were you willing to take to ensure that the identity stayed secret?

<u>Identity Discussion</u>: Why do we feel the need to keep some identities secret? Which identities are easy to talk about openly? Which are not? How can we create safe spaces where people can be honest about their identities?

Born [series]

<u>References</u>: The first three poems titled Born in this book ("Born – 1992," "Born – summer 1996," "Born – Broad Street, winter 2001") are based on a structure used by Jeanann Verlee in her work "Brawler" which can be found at http://www.radiuslit. org/2011/04/09/radius-roger-bonair-agard-jeanann-verlee-adam-falkner/. These poems were originally part of one longer poem entitled "Born" which was published in *Muzzle Magazine*.

<u>Writing Workshop</u>: These poems were written partially during a workshop led by Angel Nafis. This prompt is a modified version of that workshop. What does it mean to be reborn? Think of four

moments in your life that redefined you for a period of time. Who were you in each of these moments? Write a short paragraph for each of these different versions of yourself? Did these periods begin with pain? With love? Did they end with violence? With repentance?

Identity Discussion: When we are children we don't always understand the symbols of race, class, sexuality, gender, etc., but we are not blind to them either. How do we process these symbols? Do they look like a bodega on a summer afternoon? The first time someone called you gay? The moment you realized your shampoo was different than your friend's? What do these symbols mean? How do they still affect us today?

Broken Ghazal in the Voice of My Brother Jacob

References: To paraphrase Poets.org, the ghazal is an Arabic poetic form composed of emotionally autonomous couplets that share a refrain. Ghazals traditionally invoke love, longing, and metaphysical questions. Some ghazals that work well when teaching this are "Ghazal for My Sister" found in Angel Nafis's *BlackGirl Mansion*. More information about the ghazal form can be found at http://www.poets.org/viewmedia.php/prmMID/5781.

Writing Workshop: Make a list of words or phrases that you said or heard often when growing up. How did the meaning of these words change depending on context? List five different interpretations of one of your words or phrases. Make each interpretation a couplet in your ghazal.

Identity Discussion: How do tone and context affect our perceptions of our own identity? When you say a word associated with your identity, how is that experienced differently than when your mom says it? A friend? A bully? How do these different contexts combine to form a larger definition of these words?

Bury Me a Man

References: The villanelle is a highly structured form with 19 lines and a complex rhyme and repetition pattern. More information about the villanelle can be found here http://www.poets.org/viewmedia.php/prmMID/5796.

Writing Workshop: Write a villanelle. Think carefully about your last two lines because they will also be your first and third line and the last line of every stanza. Make sure you are repeating something worth repeating.

Identity Discussion: Troy Davis was a Black American citizen executed by the state in September 2011 after being convicted for murdering a police officer. Despite substantial evidence of innocence, the execution still took place. There is much to discuss here. Some potential topics are: state execution, the overrepresentation of Black Americans in the prison industrial complex, and current notions of safety for black males.

Covered in Grass

References: While not based on a single poem, this poem shares technique and approach with multiple poems from Tyehimba Jess's work *leadbelly*. This poem is a contrapuntal and is designed to be read down the right side independently, then the left side independently, then across.

Writing Workshop: Make a list of 5 origin stories explaining how one of your identities came to develop. Make a separate list of 5 origin stories that correspond to one of your other identities. Choose one origin story from each list and write a poem about each, simultaneously.

Identity Discussion: How do the obstacles that our ancestors overcame affect our identities today? What pains do we still carry? What have we been able to forgive?

Caprice in Elementary

<u>References</u>: This poem shares some form and structure with Jamaal May's poem "Athazagoraphobia: Fear of Being Ignored" which can be found at http://www.jamaalmay.com/published-poems/athazagoraphobia-fear-of-being-ignored/.

<u>Writing Workshop</u>: Write yourself into a childhood story that is not your own.

<u>Identity Discussion</u>: When did we learn the word gay? What did it mean when we learned it? What was the context that surrounded this education? A classroom? A school yard? How did our relationship with queerness/hetero-normativity interact with our other identities then? How does it now?

Cousin Debora Shot Herself

<u>Writing Workshop</u>: Choose a childhood event. Describe that event in the voice of a younger character present during that event. How does that character understand the event? What do they not understand?

Fire/(Fly): the Coolest Black Kid Ever

<u>Writing Workshop</u>: Make a list of people who you used to look up to but no longer do. What changed? You? Them? Describe this process.

<u>Identity Discussion</u>: How are our identities affected by those we choose to admire? How does that shift when we decide to no longer view these people as our role models?

Free to Choose

<u>References</u>: This poem is loosely based on Kevin Coval's "cracking this code" found in *L-vis Lives*.

Writing Workshop: This poem was written partially during a workshop led by Kevin Coval. This prompt is a modified version of that workshop. Make a list of the codes that you learned as a child from your neighborhood, community, culture, etc. Translate that code to your adult self.

Identity Discussion: Growing up in a neighborhood, community, culture, etc. comes with its own set of code words. Think of a time when you first saw the code and began to decipher it. What did that look like? What were the implications? How do these codes protect us? How do they hurt us?

How to Tell Your Story

References: For more information on Jewish views of the afterlife one source to read is *What Happens After I Die* by Rifat Sonsino and Daniel B. Syme.

Writing Workshop: Look at your life as if it is a narrative arc that was preplanned before you existed. How do some events in your life foreshadow other events? Choose three events that on the surface may not appear connected but are essential to the narrative of your life. How are they connected? What future events may they imply?

Identity Discussion: Many religious traditions have a belief about what happens after death. How have those beliefs impacted your identity? How do these beliefs bring us together? How do they separate us from one another?

I Watched

Writing Workshop: Make a list of 5 times you witnessed someone you care about do something that you thought was wrong but you didn't say anything to stop them. Why do we make exceptions for the people we care about? What emotional burden does this place on us?

Identity Discussion: What questionable actions do our people repeatedly engage in that we consistently find ourselves forgiving? What can those who share our identities get away with that we still hold others responsible for? Why?

Integration

Writing Workshop: Make a list of 10 ways that you are currently affected by decisions that were made one or many generations before you. How do these decisions continue to affect you today?

Identity Discussion: What identities did your parents or relatives have to keep secret in order to protect themselves? How do these secrets impact your identity today?

Jacob Taught Me

References: This poem shares some tone and structure with Michael Cirelli's "Half a Heroic Crown for Vin" found in his work *Everyone Loves The Situation* as well as at http://www.muzzlemagazine.com/michael-cirelli.html. This poem is a non-rhyming Shakespearean sonnet.

More information on sonnets can be found at http://www.poets.org/viewmedia.php/prmMID/5791.

Writing Workshop: Make a list of experiences that you shared with a friend, sibling, relative, or partner that will forever connect you to that person. Make a list of imaginary experiences that would have forever connected you to one of those people if the experience had actually occurred. Write a sonnet about one of those experiences, either true or imagined.

Identity Discussion: Our identities can be formed as much by the rules we are expected to follow as by the rules we are expected to break. What are the rules you were expected to break? How was your identity shaped when you chose to break them? When you chose not to?

Jacob Walks Home from the Providence Place Mall

References: This poem is a fictionalization of a story my brother told me about walking down Broad Street.

Writing Workshop: What is a tragic flaw? List some tragic flaws held by characters in your life. Pick one of these characters in your life and write a story exposing their tragic flaw.

Identity Discussion: What are the rules for walking home late at night as a young black male? As an adult white female? How do the rules of social behavior change depending on identity?

Kahlil Gibran Helps Aaron Reconcile the Black Penis and the Jewish Penis

References: This poem is a reworking of Kahlil Gibran's "On Joy and Sorrow" found in *The Prophet*. I reworked the poem by taking each instance of the word *joy* and replacing it with *Black Penis* and each instance of the word *sorrow* and replacing it with *Jewish Penis*. I then modified a few other places for clarity and structure. I originally was inspired to create this poem when I heard Sam Sax's poem "butthole," which was a reworking of Sylvia Plath's "Mirror" found in *Crossing the Water*. Sam Sax's poem "butthole" can be found in *Tandem* published by Bicycle Comics.

Writing Workshop: Make a list of the top ten words/concepts you always want to write about but don't feel comfortable using in your poems. Choose a poem or passage by a notable writer (Don't limit yourself. Think anything from Aristotle to Sharon Olds). Replace a few key words with one of the words from your list to change the meaning of the passage.

Identity Discussion: How are cultures reduced to certain physical stereotypes? Body parts? Speech patterns? What steps have you taken to reconcile how you actually are with the stereotypes that are thrust upon you?

Kevin Convinced Me to Drink

Writing Workshop: Make a list of ten times that you violated your own code of values. Why? Did someone convince you? Were you aware of what you were doing? How do those events connect to other times you violated your own code?

Identity Discussion: What moral obligations seem to come with our identities? Do we have additional responsibilities because of specific identities that we have? How does this affect the way we judge others? How does this affect the way we are judged?

Letter from Octavia Butler to Rabbi Moses Maimonides

References: This poem is a fictional conversation between two historical characters. Octavia Butler is a recipient of a MacArthur Fellowship, also known as a "Genius Grant", for her work as a writer, specifically works of science fiction and fantasy to chronicle the Black experience. Rabbi Moses Maimonides is a 12th century Jewish scholar who, among other accomplishments, is credited with writing down the Jewish Oral Torah and thereby being an essential component in codifying Jewish law.

Writing Workshop: Make a list of important historical figures connected to your heritage. What do they have in common? How do they differ? Have one of them write a letter to the other.

Identity Discussion: In some ways the only way to capture the ridiculousness of oppression is by veering towards the absurd. What are absurd examples of oppression that still affect us today? How are they often discussed?

Mom Explains the Events that Took Place after Her Father Died

References: The epigraph to this poem is from Daphne Gottlieb's "the jewish atheist mother has her say" which can be found in her work *Why Things Burn* as well as at http://www.daphnegottlieb.com/poems.html.

<u>Writing Workshop</u>: Sometimes our true, lived experiences are more unbelievable than anything we could imagine. Make a list of five true stories from your own life that sound so ridiculous when you tell them that nobody believes they actually happened. Choose one to write a poem about.

<u>Identity Discussion</u>: How has family lore affected your perception of what can be true? What legends were passed down to you from your relatives? What was true? Untrue? Does it matter?

Miriam's Apology

<u>References</u>: This poem is a retelling of the story where Miriam places Moses in a basket, which is a story from the book of Exodus in the Hebrew Bible. In this story the Egyptian pharaoh had ordered that all newborn Jewish males be killed. To save Moses, his older sister Miriam places him in a basket and sends him down a river. He is discovered and adopted by an Egyptian princess and is raised as a prince among Egyptian royalty.

<u>Writing Workshop</u>: Think of the stories you were told in your childhood, from fables to television shows to family lore. Who was the protagonist? Who were the supporting characters? Rewrite this story from the perspective of one of the supporting characters.

<u>Identity Discussion</u>:   Many stories tell of a protagonist who is able to jump social classes. One of the reasons this phenomenon has been glorified is because of its rarity. How do we perceive our own class? Compared to our parents? Grandparents? Have you/your family changed your social class? How? Why?

My Grandma

<u>Writing Workshop</u>: Make a list of five people in your life who would never brag about how awesome they are. Choose one. Make a list of ten ways that person is awesome. Write a poem that tells the world how awesome that person is.

<u>Identity Discussion</u>: What are the battles that our grandparents had to fight that we don't have to fight? Our great-grandparents? What are the battles that we share? How are these related to our identity?

Palmalysis

<u>Writing Workshop</u>: What are some phenomena that you have experienced but that do not have a definition? Describe them. Write the dictionary definition.

<u>Identity Discussion</u>: What are some moments where you have felt paralyzed in a social setting? How was this social paralysis related to one of your identities? What were some of your thoughts? How did you move forward?

Peter is Dead and I am a Motorcycle

<u>References</u>: This poem references The Station nightclub fire, which is one of the most deadly nightclub fires in U.S. history. The Station was a rock and roll night club located in West Warwick, Rhode Island. There were over 100 fatalities.

<u>Writing Workshop</u>: Make a list of five moments during which you were forced to grow up. What did each moment look like? Make a list of one object that stands out in your memory as the definitive image of each moment. Write about one of these images.

Promises

<u>References</u>: I attribute the epigraph in this poem to Albert Einstein. I grew up thinking Einstein said this quote. However, after further research, it appears that there is no concrete evidence to prove that Einstein was the quote's originator.

<u>Writing Workshop</u>: Make a list of five phrases that you were told repeatedly while you were growing up. In what context were these phrases said? What did they mean? Choose one and use it as a refrain in a poem.

Pulling

<u>References</u>: While not based on a single poem, this poem shares technique and approach with multiple poems from M.A. Vizsolyi's work *The Lamp with Wings*. This poem is a non-rhyming Shakespearean sonnet. More information on sonnets can be found at http://www.poets.org/viewmedia.php/prmMID/5791.

<u>Writing Workshop</u>: Sometimes we have memories that we know can't possibly be true, but we have the memories none the less. Are we remembering a dream? Are we just manufacturing a memory because it is better than the truth? Make a list of five moments you remember that can't possibly be true. Write yourself back into one of those memories, or all of them.

<u>Identity Discussion</u>: How are we allowed to love? Not allowed to love? What are the rules of love that are dictated by our identities?

Rules

<u>Writing Workshop</u>: What are the unwritten rules in your culture, neighborhood, gender, race, class, identity, etc.? Diagram them into a poem.

<u>Identity Discussion</u>: How are our actions dictated by the unwritten rules that come with our identities? How do they impact the way we interact with one another?

Shabbat Shalom: the Coolest Jewish Kid Ever

<u>References</u>: This poem shares some form and approach with Patrick Rosal's "Beast" found in *My American Kundiman* as well as at http://www.oovrag.com/poems/poems2008b-rosal2.shtml.

<u>Writing Workshop</u>: Make a list of your heroes in your respective identity categories. Who defined your gender for you? Who defined your race? Who was the epitome of one of your identities? This could be a fictional character, best friend, professional athlete, etc. Describe them. What was the secret to their magic?

<u>Identity Discussion</u>: How do we try to live up to the standards set by our heroes? How do we fail? What does this failure imply about our identities?

Special Delivery: the Blackest Jewish Kid Ever

<u>References</u>: This poem is based on Jon Sands's poem "Party & Bullshit" found in *The New Clean* as well as at http://www.youtube.com/watch?v=4Dgn0uBcOGw. Jon Sands's poem is based on the Biggie Smalls song, "Party and Bullshit," which was the artist's debut single.

<u>Writing Workshop</u>: What song makes you feel like the coolest person in the world when you listen to it? Listen to this song on repeat while you write this poem. Find a moment where you were the coolest version of yourself. Take us to this moment.

<u>Identity Discussion</u>: How do we perform for our peers in order to belong? Does this involve practice or preparation? Does a successful performance succeed in making us feel like we belong or do we need to continually perform?

Tashlikh

References: This poem shares form and structure with Joy Harjo's poem "Deer Dancer" which can be found at http://www.poets.org/viewmedia.php/prmMID/15475.

Writing Workshop: Make a list of five people you love. Next to each person, list a moment when you were furious with that person. Next to each person, list a moment when you were most overcome with love for that person. They can be the same moment, or different moments. Choose one person and write a poem that brings the reader on a journey from the first moment to the second moment.

Identity Discussion: How is our identity dependent on tradition? If we fail to uphold a tradition connected to our identity, do we fail as members of that identity category?

Ten Plagues

References: This poem is based on a structure used by Laura Yes Yes in her poem "College Transcript" found in *How to Seduce a White Boy in Ten Easy Steps*.

Writing Workshop: There are many examples of instructions that can be found in our culture and heritage. This could be anything from the Ten Commandments to a cooking recipe. Make a list of one particular set of instructions connected to your identity. Interpret this list with the voice of the culture from which it comes. Interpret it through a different voice. How do the voices talk to each other?

Identity Discussion: The word terrorism is sometimes applied to people who harm innocent civilians in order to advance a political agenda. However, many people now considered heroes and freedom fighters were labeled as terrorists in their time. What makes someone a terrorist? Is violence ever an acceptable political tactic?

The Black Penis Talks Shit to the Rest of Aaron
& The Jewish Penis Talks Shit to the Rest of Aaron

References: These poems are based on the form and structure of multiple poems that invoke the concept of playing the dozens. Two poems that I model heavily are "Angel's Heart Clowns the Ocean," found in Angel Nafis's *BlackGirl Mansion* and "snaps! L-vis learns to play the dozens" found in Kevin Coval's *L-vis Lives*.

Writing Workshop: The game of playing the dozens is popular in black communities and involves insulting one another in an attempt to constantly one-up the competitor. These games often involve 'yo momma' jokes. What happens when you play the dozens with yourself? Pick one of your identities and have it play the dozens with another one of your identities.

Identity Discussion: How do our identities come into conflict within ourselves? How is this reinforced by external influences? What can we do to reconcile this internal conflict?

The Multiracial Asian German Woman

Writing Workshop: Make a list of five times you have been absolutely overcome with hatred. Choose one. What drove you to hatred? How did you react? How does this moment compare to other similar moments where you were more forgiving or understanding?

Identity Discussion: Sometimes we choose to embrace hatred while other times we are more forgiving or understanding. Why do we choose to be forgiving in some instances and not others? How does our identity contribute to this? How does the identity of the object of our hatred contribute to this?

The Worst Parts of Love

References: This poem is based on the form and structure of Jeanann Verlee's "and/or" found in *Racing Hummingbirds*.

<u>Writing Workshop</u>: For this prompt, give yourself permission to write down things that you will not share with anyone. Write down ten things you have done that scare you. Why do they scare you? What are you afraid of? Write a poem that scares you. Do not share it. Edit it until you are ready to share it. Or never share it.

<u>Identity Discussion</u>: How do implicit power dynamics affect our relationships with one another? How can we recognize when we are in a position of power? When we are not? What responsibilities come with these positions? What fears come with these positions?

Totem: Malcolm X Dog Tag

<u>Writing Workshop</u>: A totem is an object that serves as an emblem or a signifier, often as a reminder of heritage. Totems can be used to anchor an individual to some aspect of their reality. Make a list of ten totems that you have used in your life to assert an aspect of your identity. Why did you feel the need to use them? What was their magic? Choose one and write a poem about its power.

<u>Identity Discussion</u>: Sometimes we use totems to prove to others some aspect of our identity. Sometimes we use them to prove aspects of our identity to ourselves. What totems have you used in your life to assert your identity? How have you used them? Did it work?

Translating Jacob

<u>References</u>: This poem is based on a structure used by Jeanann Verlee in her work "Poem to Translate the Poems" which can be found at http://www.failbetter.com/42/VerleePoem.php.

<u>Writing Workshop</u>: This poem was written during a workshop led by Angel Nafis. This prompt is a modified version of that workshop. Make a list of the five most defining moments of your childhood. Now choose one of those events. Make a list of 10 images or actions that took place during this event. Now define each of these images or actions using only language from this event. Now weave these definitions together to create a poem that defines the event itself.

What Really Happened on Mt. Moriah

References: This poem is a retelling of the "The Binding of Isaac" which is a story from the book of *Genesis* in the Hebrew Bible. In this story God commands Abraham to sacrifice his son Isaac as a demonstration his faith. Just as Abraham is about to kill his son, an angel comes from the heavens and stops him, offering a ram to be sacrificed instead. Many rabbis, scholars, and philosophers have written commentary on this story. Some are heavily critical while others praise this story as a testament to the power of faith. One of the most notable writings on this story is by philosopher Søren Kierkegaard in his work *Fear and Trembling*.

Writing Workshop: Think of the stories you were told in your childhood, from fables to television shows to family lore. What was problematic about these stories? What lessons did they teach that you disagree with? Pick one of these stories and retell it, changing just a few crucial details to give the story a different meaning.

Identity Discussion: How are we shaped by the stories we are told as children? Share some stories that were supposed to teach us a lesson as children. What do we agree with? Disagree with? How are these stories affected by race, class, gender, sexuality, and our other identities?

When Moses Stayed

References: This poem was inspired by Kevin Coval's poem "When Ismael Comes Home" in his work *What I Will Tell My Jewish Kids*.

Writing Workshop: Make a list of people connected to your history who had taboo or unexpected relationships: best friends, partners, spouses, and children. Choose one. Why was this relationship a deviation from the norm? What obstacles did they have to overcome?

Identity Discussion: Why is so much time spent on policing who we are allowed to love? Be friends with? Where does this pressure come from? Does it protect us? Does it hurt us?

Why Moses Left

References: This poem is a reinterpretation of the story of Moses and the burning bush from the book of *Exodus* in the Hebrew Bible. In this story Moses is content with his new life away from Egypt. God speaks to Moses through a burning bush in order to convince him to return to Egypt to free his people from slavery.

Writing Workshop: Think of a fantastic story from your own life or connected to your heritage. Write the story with no fantasy. Remove the magic from the story and see what is left.

Identity Discussion: Do we have an obligation to people just because they share an identity with us (race, gender, orientation, family)? If so, where does this obligation come from? When have we neglected it?

Which Keeps Me

References: This poem is based on a structure used by Jeanann Verlee in her work "Poem to Translate the Poems" which can be found at http://www.failbetter.com/42/VerleePoem.php.

Writing Workshop: This poem was written during a workshop led by Angel Nafis. This prompt is a modified version of that workshop. When you think about your heritage, write down the first ten images that come to your mind. What do they mean? Why do you continue to return to these images? Define these images. Write a poem that connects these definitions in order to build a larger definition of one aspect of your identity.

Identity Discussion: Why is identity so difficult to define? What are the symbols that we associate with who we are? Food? Colors? Textures? Music? When do these symbols of identity interact in harmony with each other? When do they conflict? How does that harmony or conflict affect our interactions with one another?

While Waiting for the Messiah

Writing Workshop: Make a list of ten dead people that you would like to have a casual conversation with. Choose one. What would you discuss? What would you choose not to discuss?

Identity Discussion: Who are you waiting for? Who is your family waiting for? What is supposed to change upon their arrival? How do we define ourselves by the things that are absent from our lives?

Why Jewish Kids Ain't White Sometimes

References: This poem shares a structure used by Willie Perdomo in his work "Nigger-Reecan Blues" which can be found at http://www. youtube.com/watch?v=7An4hEmRHTk. The poem also draws in tone and style from the Thomas Sayers Ellis poem "Or" found in his work *Skin, Inc.* as well as at http://www.poetryfoundation.org/ poetrymagazine/poem/178676.

Writing Workshop: This poem was written during a workshop led by Kevin Coval. This prompt is a modified version of that workshop. Make a list of ten of your identities. Now make a list of ten quotes people have said to you that made you question the validity of one of these identities. Write.

Identity Discussion: Identity can be influenced by the way we feel about ourselves as well as the way that other people feel about us. Which of these has been more influential in the way you identify? How does that importance differ based on each specific identity?

For more information about facilitating a writing workshop or identity discussion based on these poems, please contact me at AaronSamuelsPoetry.com.

ACKNOWLEDGEMENTS

Many thanks to the journals in which the poems below first appeared, some in different versions:

Apogee Journal: "Letter from Octavia Butler to Rabbi Moses Maimonides"

Mandala Journal: "When Moses Didn't Come Home"

Muzzle Magazine: "Born," "Which Keeps Me"

Radius: "Born," "Broken Ghazal in the Voice of My Brother Jacob," "Kevin Convinced Me to Drink"

Sole Literary Journal: "Tashlikh"

The Nervous Breakdown: "The Worst Parts of Love"

The Tidal Basin Review: "Bury Me a Man"

Thrush Poetry Journal: "Translating Jacob"

Union Station Magazine: "Fire/(Fly): the Coolest Black Kid Ever," "How to Tell Your Story"

Used Furniture Review: "Free to Choose," "Mom Explains the Events that Took Place after Her Father Died," "Palmalysis"

THANK YOU

To Laura Yes Yes. This book would not exist without you. I look up to you hellaz and it has been a privilege to work with you through this process. Thank you for pushing me.

To Geoff Kagan-Trenchard and Emily Kagan-Trenchard, for inviting me and my manuscript into your home, and for feeding both of us.

To Jon Sands, for the ridiculously close reads, and constant feedback.

To Jeanann Verlee, for making me feel welcome in the New York poetry community, and for writing incredible work that inspired so many of these poems.

To Jared Paul. You will always be my coach.

To Jamila Woods, Nate Marshall, Franny Choi, Fatimah Asghar, and Danez Smith, for marching next to me.

To Lauren Banka, for your friendship, guidance, and commitment to my growth. And for the amazing cover art.

To Heidi Durrow and Darryl Wash, for making my success your priority.

To Jared Singer and James Merenda, for welcoming me to the party with open arms.

To Audrey Samuels, Laura Levy, Helga Samuels. Thank you for being my Grandmas. You have carried so much.

To Sandra Levy, Robert Samuels, and Devin Samuels, for being with me every step of the way. I love you.

To Edgewood, especially: Patrick Stycos, Jeff Denault, Glenn McGillivray, Will Kelleher, and Chris Horvat.

To Millbrook 302, specifically: Pierre Boncy, Adrian Githuku, Joshua Trupman, Chris Rodgers, Uche Onwuzurike, and Roger Murayi.

To my fantastic editors, mentors, and friends, for essential support throughout the process: Corey Coleman, Gahl Liberzon, Mikkel Snyder, Lucy Gellman, Laura Brown-Lavoie, Stevie Edwards, Aimeé Lê, Lynne Procope, Jezra Kaye, Jeff Kass, Kevin Coval, Karen Kalish, Kim Frisch, Leah Nixon, Celso White, Chris Kammerer, Eric Rosenbaum, Max Kessler, Fiona Chamness, Meg Fogarty, Phil Kaye, Jamie Kaye-Phillips, Zack Jackson, Max McFadden, Alex Kiles, Monica Smith, Kate Gaertner, Sophie Adelman, Nate Maslak, Alex Greenberg, Rachel Bader, Crystal Spence, Arianna Foster, Jessica Spraos, AJ Krebs, Carrie Rudzinski, Angel Nafis, Sam Sax, Chinaka Hodge.

To the communities that nurtured and supported my development: WU-SLam, Providence Poetry Slam, Volume Summer Institute, Cultural Leadership, Louder Arts, Urbana Poetry Slam, Be'chol Lashon, and Cave Canem.

To Derrick Brown and the Write Bloody Family. Thank you for believing in my work.

ABOUT THE AUTHOR

Aaron Samuels is a native of Edgewood, Rhode Island, and a Cave Canem Fellow. His work has been nominated for a Pushcart Prize and appeared in *The Tidal Basin Review, Used Furniture Review, Muzzle Magazine*, and *Thrush Poetry Journal*, among others. Aaron was featured on the debut episode of TV One's *Verses & Flow*, and his work has been featured at *TEDx Washington University*, HBO's *Brave New Voices*, and the *Mixed Roots Film & Literary Festival*. He is the founder of Washington University Poetry Slam, known throughout St. Louis for its literacy development work at local high schools, juvenile detention centers, and community organizations. *Yarmulkes & Fitted Caps* is Aaron's first full length poetry collection.

Come say hi at *AaronSamuelsPoetry.com*.

If You Like Aaron Levy Samuels, Aaron Levy Samuels Likes...

How to Seduce a White Boy in Ten Easy Steps
Laura Yes Yes

These Are the Breaks
Idris Goodwin

Racing Hummingbirds
Jeananne Verlee

The New Clean
Jon Sands

Good Grief
Stevie Edwards

What the Night Demands
Miles Walser

Write Bloody Publishing distributes and promotes great books of fiction, poetry and art every year. We are an independent press dedicated to quality literature and book design, with an office in Austin, TX.

Our employees are authors and artists so we call ourselves a family. Our design team comes from all over America: modern painters, photographers and rock album designers create book covers we're proud to be judged by.

We publish and promote 8-12 tour-savvy authors per year. We are grass-roots, D.I.Y., bootstrap believers. Pull up a good book and join the family. Support independent authors, artists and presses.

**Want to know more about Write Bloody books, authors and events?
Join our maling list at**

www.writebloody.com

WRITE BLOODY BOOKS

CPSIA information can be obtained
at www.ICGtesting.com
Printed in the USA
FSOW01n1658021215
13728FS

9 781938 912382